Tending Your Inner Garden®

Summer

Women's Writings for the
Season of Beauty and Resilience

Edited by Debra Landwehr Engle
and Diane Glass

First GoldenTree Communications Edition June 2013

© 2013 by Tending Your Inner Garden®

Publisher and Editors: Debra Landwehr Engle, Diane Glass
Cover design: Wendy Musgrave
Editor photographs © Amy Allen and Flash Digital Photos

Printed in the United States of America
by MacDonald Letter Service

ISBN 978-0-9894037-3-3 soft cover
GoldenTree Communications, LLC
Winterset, Iowa

To our mothers,
who encouraged us to write.

❧

Acknowledgments

As we publish the third of our series of books honoring the seasons of the year, we're delighted to see the impact of encouraging women to write their stories and share them with the world.

One of our authors has since published a memoir. Another proudly promotes her writing by acknowledging her published essay on her web site. Several authors have submitted subsequent work for this volume. New writers have sought us out. Readers tell us they have been moved, entertained, surprised, affirmed and informed by the efforts of these women.

These books continue to be a team effort. We thank Wendy Musgrave for her exceptional cover art and Christina Baldwin and Jennifer Louden for lending their valued endorsements. Most of all, we thank all the writers who submitted their work for this volume, lending their voices to uplift women everywhere.

Contents

Introduction

I: JOY

II: STORMS

III: MINDFULNESS

IV: RESILIENCE

V: BEAUTY

ॐ

Introduction

Summer blesses us with both gifts and challenges. Riotous color and parched grassland. Thunderous storms and blissful sunny days. Hot, buggy evenings and cool early mornings. Kaleidoscope-like butterflies and ravenous locusts. Most of us welcome summer if for no other reason than it surprises us year after year.

Summer: Women's Writings for the Season of Beauty and Resilience will delight you with the adventures it offers and the memories it evokes.

Companion a hiker as she is "forced to pay attention to every step" on a climb near Glacier National Park.

Open your heart to a grandmother who recalls her own summer barefoot childhood as she shares a beach adventure with her granddaughter.

Empathize with the resilience of a gardener who fought the bugs and worms in her garden by learning to work with nature, rather than resist it.

Listen to the warm remembrances of an ex-wife who decides to share stories only she knows at her former husband's funeral.

Read the tender account of a woman who loses her baby in the womb.

Recall your own experience of hanging the wash with clothespins—or discover it for the first time.

"Now is the season to call back your heart," Celeste Snowber tells us in "Bodypsalm for Playing." This volume will help you do so by evoking feelings associated with both storms and resilience, beauty and mindfulness. Then take pen and paper and use the journaling questions at the end of the book to capture your own memories of summer.

—*Debra Landwehr Engle and Diane Glass*
www.tendingyourinnergarden.com

I.

J O Y

&

❧

Pat Made Me Do It.
Or Maybe It Was the Chicken

By Mary Cartledgehayes

One evening in the summer of 2012 my friend Pat Jobe posted a blip on Facebook saying, "Write a hundred words on *oneness*."

I don't know that the blip was intended for me. Possibly it was a generic stab-in-the-dark, let's-get-some-spiritual-growth-going-here adventure with which Pat was experimenting. I could have ignored him, engrossed as I was in the women's track and field events at the London Olympics, but Pat is an old friend. Not only that, he once wrote a song based on a story he heard from a man who got annoyed while getting the table ready for a picnic. Really annoyed. Heaving-plates-up-against-the-barn-wall-and-breaking-them annoyed.

Next thing he knew, he had a headache, and an obviously miffed chicken (I'm picturing a white Leghorn) was stomping off across the barnyard.

The plate-throwing man was baffled by this turn of events until he heard his wife's voice behind him.

"Now throw another plate," she drawled, slowly.

Experience shows that any number of people can tell an adequate chicken-pitching story, but Pat Jobe is the genius who can write a song about it, accompany himself on a guitar while singing and taping it, and then load the finished video onto youtube so you can see and hear him sing.

With his song, Pat reawakened my sense of the possibilities inherent in poetry, not to mention in poultry. I felt as though I needed to return Pat's favor somehow, and therefore I offered him, in a burst of understanding and gratitude toward my younger self, the following one hundred words.

Oneness
Seeing the women win big at the Olympics
I'm knowing we did that. We, feminists
working as one in committees on phone trees
on congressional visits on letters

at our homes and at our meetings and
our marches, for years.
We, working, toward one goal: that our daughters,
our granddaughters, everybody's granddaughters,
girls and women, through every generation
might stand on a stage, around her neck a ribbon draped
at the bottom of which gold silver bronze hangs heavy
while "The Star-Spangled Banner"
plays for her, for us.

If you love those Olympic champions
with their medals, laughter, nosegays,
thank one feminist tomorrow.
You're welcome.

By now, the word count may not conform to Pat's desire for 100 words. I've meddled with it, tidied up a misplaced modifier, made improvements. At the time, you see, it was a toss-off, a blip, not so different from a summer love born of propinquity and the flickering light of a television set.

Today, though, I remembered my hundred words on oneness, and I thought, "Yes. I want the idea to circulate in print, electronically, that we women throw chickens, and that we women work for and achieve opportunity, justice and greatness—and that we women stand proudly on the platform, gold silver bronze medals aglow under the lights.

Too Young to Be Old

By Phyllis Jardine

At fifty you promised twenty more years together.

Those twenty years have come and gone, dear love.

Years with Friday-night dates and a cottage by the sea.

Will you give me twenty more years, dear love?

Twenty years to romp and play, to dance and sing?

Growing old frightens me, dear love.

But the time will come, I know.

Will you walk me through those years?

Can we climb life's stairs together?

Life has given us many gifts, dear love:

A country road to embrace us,

A faithful dog to walk us,

A mile of sand to sift our troubles,

Thin places to nurture us,

Grandchildren's laughter to soften us.

We've already lived a lifetime, love.

So when ninety comes with her aches and pains,

When our days shorten and our vision blurs,

Will you promise me—with your embraces, your teasing,

Your secret words of endearment,

That Insha'llah—if God is willing,

We'll be okay, dear love?

Because, we're too young to be old.

When He Looked Like James Dean

By Terri Elders

When I walked into the foyer of the Little Brown Church for Bob's memorial service, I broke into a grin. Our son, Steve, had posted a blown-up photograph of his dad. Bob, at 19, shrugging into a leather flight jacket, eyes squinting against smoke from his Corona, looking jauntily suave, the perfect embodiment of early '50s cool.

We'd been divorced for nearly twenty-five years. In fact, when Steve called me, while he related the details, I did the math. *If* we hadn't been divorced back in 1980, *if* we'd remained in our genial but increasingly disunited marriage, and *if* Bob hadn't succumbed to lung cancer, on June 18th we'd celebrate our golden anniversary.

Though I'd not seen my ex since I'd remarried five years earlier, I'd continued to send greeting cards. I knew of Bob's hospitalizations and that over the past few years he'd lost nearly seventy pounds. Steve said he looked closer to 85 than his actual age of 73.

Now, staring at the photo of the Bob of my youth, I remembered how we'd met. In 1954 I'd been editor of the community college paper, and Bob, a Korean War vet attending on the GI Bill, had been taking a photography class. Since the photo lab was housed in the journalism building, Bob used to joke about trying to lure me into the darkroom.

Seated in the chapel, I listened as my son welcomed the crowds who had come to celebrate his father's life. Steve spoke of finding the photo in the foyer, how astonished he'd been to discover how *cool* Bob looked, and how he'd looked like James Dean even *before* Dean became a star. The audience chuckled.

Then Steve mentioned how his father had been smart enough to marry not one, but two, smart women. I heard somebody in the back whisper, "I wonder if Terri's here."

As others talked of their memories, I reflected on how our divorce had opened doors for both of us. Bob had found a more compatible woman, one who shared his interests, which involved recovery programs right in the town where he'd been born.

Our divorce had released me geographically so that I could work with the Peace Corps. I'd heard gray wolves howl on the spring equinox in Mongolia, stared down a baby octopus while snorkeling in Seychelles' warm Indian Ocean waters, dined on armadillo at Macy's Café in Belize. I'd explored the Toledo, the castle in Spain I'd dreamed of since childhood.

Whenever I visited California, Bob would take me to lunch and listen to my adventures.

Steve asked if anybody else wanted to speak. I rose, approached the dais, and heard somebody exclaim, "Why, it's Terri."

"With the exception of his niece, I've known Bob longer than anybody here today," I began.

Then I told of our first encounter. After I'd exited from a Western Civilization test in late 1954, Bob gave me a wolf whistle. I walked over and said, "That's cheered me up." I stood on tiptoe and gave him a peck on his cheek.

Bob grinned and said, "If I get that for a whistle, I'm going home and get my bugle." The audience roared.

I recounted Bob's earlier achievements, emphasized he'd been the quintessential optimist and vouched that he indeed had been cool. "I'm happy to say," I concluded, "that I knew Bob Elders when he looked like James Dean."

Not long after, I found an abelia shrub called Golden Anniversary. Bob and I had been married for only twenty-five years, but had remained friends for an additional twenty-five. That chilly June 18th, I planted the Golden Anniversary.

Bodypsalm for Playing

By Celeste Snowber

What ever happened
to the sheer delight of
p l a y i n g
where your fingers and feet
touch the earth
and you play in the mud
let sand run through your palms
and sea, salt and dirt glide
on the edge of your skin

remember the joy of
rinsing your hair in the rain
and running through an open field
and dancing on the shores

of the body of water
you knew as a child

Why does Jesus say
you must be like a child
to come into the kin(g)dom of heaven
fresh and fragrant
is the place
to play and pray
in dusk and dawn

Now is the season
to call back your heart
to live with lightness
and cherish the chance
to take back what you deeply know
find the joy in movements
which sweep your being
into first utterance

the sound of words falling from breath

the touch of wet sand on arms

the scent of sky

the dance of wind

Reinhabit

the ecstatic pause

where play takes up its vital cause

and you answer

YES!

Nikola

by Phyllis Jardine

I see her zooming over the hill on her bike, pajamas flying in the breeze, helmet hanging loosely over uncombed hair, bare feet dangling in the dirt.

There goes my quiet walk down to the beach—the place where I release the pressures and worries of the day. But time and grandchildren have softened my edges, so I follow Nikola down through the woods. It's daybreak and we're going kayaking in the cove.

Flashes of another barefoot summer cross my mind: I'm visiting my grandmother and sleeping under the stars with her, my aunt and my little brother. I was about five years old. My grandmother would have been in her seventies, my age today. I remember discovering the magic of fireflies in her backyard that summer. How, like magic, they would rise to the top of the trees and garland the branches like twinkling stars.

This morning Nikola and I hurry to gather our own magic from a summer that is still ours to enjoy. She runs through the woods along a zigzagging path and onto beach pebbles that I feel even through my Holy Soles beach clogs.

The summer sun peeks through the fog as Nikola and I sail into the quiet, cruising the bay. I look at this mite of a girl and wonder if she's quiet because she's as enthralled as I am by the sound of the sea, the sense of freedom and the remoteness of this place. Or if she's like the wind, sometimes happy, sometimes sad? Perhaps she's just tired, allowing her mind to wander, to daydream.

"Woolgathering," my grandmother used to say, "is good for the soul." I honor Nikola's silence. There's another old truth that says every cell in our body changes every seven years. Is Nikola in a state of flux? Is she, like me, facing a new stage of growth? Will she one day look back and remember snatched fragments of the sweetness of our time together?

After about an hour we paddle towards the calm surf where the water isn't going anywhere, neither coming in or going out—ebb tide. Or as my navy husband calls it, neap tide—a less than average high tide, occurring at the first and third quarter of the moon. There's no arriving, just becoming. Something serene in me tells me we don't have to circumvent the globe to find inner peace; we simply need to cruise the bay.

I glance in Nikola's direction. Held by the hand of God, with tongue clenched firmly between loose baby teeth, she doesn't fit the part of a seasoned sailor, but she turns her kayak around and comes alongside me, her beautiful smile melting the morning's mist.

A girl and her boat, out here in the wilderness, with the sea-wind blowing in her hair. *Time for breakfast,* I whisper to Nikola as a warm breeze, like a pair of old arms that will never hold me again, tightens around me, soft and silent forever.

We haul the boats up to higher ground and, overwhelmed by the power of remembrance, I take her hand in mine and say the words my grandmother used to say to me: "I don't know what I'd do without you, dear."

~

Urie's Fish Bait

By Mari Wetter

Urie's Fish Bait sign

an unblinking eye

a great beacon from across the bay.

Countless summers at the Jersey Shore

we walked miles for a dead head wrapped in newsprint

with which many crabs to lure

stinking and rotting yet serene,

a meditation of wandering over the connecting bridge

while the two gate-men ushered us along,

guardians to the sea vessels weighing 1000s of times their

weight,

Pat Boone writing us "Love Letters" while we scuffled

after crabs just the right size and sex,

five-inch males with lots of flesh,

a gourmet meal for less than a dime.

We were rich and richer because we had the time

to tell secrets and jokes and swish the sand under the
bulkhead
where the shadows cooled the sand and fooled our prey,
so moist and delicately buttery.
They gave us a quarter and since fish heads only cost a
nickel,
we split the change.
In the summer seasons it rattles my Keds,
a forever sweet season in my heart and my head.

Tracing the Goddess

By Ann Quid

A woman alive
knows the truth in her smallest bones
every tooth, eyelash
and whispering nodule
of her most excellent body

She carries a stone-filled urn
to the fountains
trading rock for juicy, clear
remembrance of water's greatest gift:
the passage of the babe

She employs a savory liking
for bodacious, resolved to declare
the decencies deserved

and knows the precision and covert strength
it takes to walk peacefully
without rancor
on this plane of living.

Only tomorrow
fresh with promise
compares to what woman
has gleaned this day

Feisty eternal warp of moon
The sun's golden hour
The breath between the two.

II.

STORMS

❧

Illumination

By Ronda Armstrong

Clouds darken.
    Storms hover.
        Rain splatters.
            Lightning streaks.
                Thunder cracks.
Sunlight within
    turns on
        to answer
        nature's calls
            to lead.

                    Hearts swell
           with thanks
        for storms that
      rock life's rhythm,
              that teeter between
        life's Yes
and the dark spots
that illumine us,
        that propel us forward
             when perhaps we
would   just stay put
        to lie in darkness.

"Feelings, Whoa, Whoa, Whoa Feelings..."

By Susan Wilson

Some days feel lousy; one of them caught up with me. It was a horrible, terrible, no good, very bad day. My body ached, and my legs refused to move beyond a plodding walk. Tears flowed at the speed I wished my legs would move. I felt so tired, and betrayed by the pain running through my body.

That night, my husband and I gathered with our Community Group, a group who lives and loves through life together. We each make the commitment to show up with honesty, love, and present-moment living. Before opening the door to our host's home, I took a deep breath and planted a smile on my face, remembering, "You're never fully dressed without a smile." (Uh huh, I feel the irony too).

After dinner, we stayed at the table to dive into our discussion with Brené Brown's, *The Gifts of Imperfection*. Our chapter, "Cultivating Authenticity: Letting Go of What People Think," ended with the final question, "How do you DIG deep?" an invitation to:

Get *Deliberate* about remaining authentic vs. shrinking or throwing up defensive armor when we feel vulnerable.

Get *Inspired* by staying open to others' courage as encouragement for our own.

Get *Going,* with vulnerability *and* authenticity sharing space.

With Brené's ideas seeking a place in my emotional space, I heard, "Susan, what about you?"

"Excuse me?"

"What about Brené's question, "How do you DIG deep—get deliberate, get inspired and get going?"

One of the men added, "Like with your cancer...."

I opened my mouth to describe how cancer has deepened my faith and expanded my understanding of love. Then I paused.

An echo to "show up and be real in this present moment" asked for attention. The smile that dressed my face with words to back it up changed. Fresh words tumbled: "I don't know. Right now, I hurt. I want to feel positive, but I don't. I don't want to pray. I feel tired. And I'm tired of pain that lives with me. I hate whining, but there it is."

Though I felt pangs of guilt for giving voice to "negative" feelings, I also felt relief in the release of real feelings that most often stay tucked away. I didn't focus on my "best foot forward." Instead, I held what we, as a group, say is most important—honesty, love, and present-moment living. As I surveyed the faces and saw that they simply listened, I relaxed.

Were those minutes life-changing? Will I be that forthcoming forevermore? I wish I could say "yes." However, I did feel my perspective shift. I took a risk (my choice) and experienced a community of people who listened with a spirit of acceptance (their choice). A "next time" will come with that group—another invitation to risk with honest expression of feelings. It won't feel as scary.

Most of us want listening that accepts who we are right now. "Appropriate at all times" is not a sustainable way of life. We seek space for authenticity—to show up, speak up, and then shut up to rest with our thoughts and feelings (sometimes accompanied by tear-up healing water).

Most of us value thoughtful advice and help with problems. We feel more receptive when our emotional soil is fertile, not fatigued. Inclusive silence with loving acceptance of who we are and where we are "in this moment" nurtures essential fertility.

When we risk honest expression in courage, we yearn for others to *encourage* with listening that seeks to understand. Can each of us be one of those "others?"

∾

First Child

By Kirsten LaBlanc

I lay back and absorbed the icy gel on my belly while my husband stood close by. I heard my child's heartbeat. LUB DUB LUB DUB. Relief.

"I'm going to do some measurements." The tech typed as she spoke. "When did you say you last had a period?" She made some notes. "I see." She stopped writing and she stopped typing. The world paused with her. "The heartbeat is a bit slow. Maybe you aren't as far along as you thought?"

Could have been. Maybe.

"Sometimes these things are complicated," she said as her eyes melted into mine. Her kindness became more apparent. "I'm going to have the doctor come in now to discuss the results. Please stay here. I won't be long."

We stayed, and after what seemed like three days later, she returned. "You can get dressed now."

28

She led us to an office where we were met by a man, presumably the doctor, and a younger resident. I cannot tell you if the resident was a he or a she. I do not remember. I do remember coming home and Scott calling the family. I understood what was happening and that I would return to the hospital in three days for another ultrasound and more bloodwork. I used that time to convince myself everything was fine.

Three days later, we knew for sure nothing was fine. I held my breath as the tech searched for that heartbeat. Nothing. No one could tell me what to expect next. I needed to know. I spoke only to a few close relatives: my husband, my sister. I spoke to my mom to tell her this grandchild was not to be, and we cried together. Separated by 637 miles, yet we were joined as one in the bond of motherhood.

My body had a two-week deadline before the procedure would be necessary. My body felt no urgency and waited exactly 14 days. The few people who knew told me it was over. Now I could move on and try again.

Except, it wasn't and I couldn't. My emotions were compounded by a coworker's growing belly. Her due date was the same as mine. As her belly grew, my darkness followed. I was consumed. By the time November came, my tears were constant. I counted the days. December 10 burned in my heart. I couldn't keep on this path, and I didn't know if there was another to take.

How do you tell someone you are grieving a child you never held? You don't. Instead, you keep the secret so as not to worry relatives. You think about the missing headstone and wonder if your child's soul was baptized by love.

After a while, you wonder if you are "normal." If you aren't, will you ever be? You beg for peace and plead for closure. Then you wonder why God hasn't responded.

I found an email address for my pastor and used it. We prayed together seeking peace. She gave me permission to be angry with God. I was. She asked me to start an honest dialogue. I spoke nonstop for two hours, pausing only to cry and to laugh. My pastor gave the insanity a name. It was called grief. I was the same as any parent who had lost a child. Even though I felt that I had no right to mourn, exhaustion had taken a toll and I no longer had a fighting spirit. I gave in. I wept. I began to heal.

↷

Meeting Kelly

By Geri Moran

I was at another of life's crossroads, unemployed after losing a job I loved, alone, depressed, and feeling unable to rise to another challenge. I decided to take some of my meager savings and flee to Mystic, Connecticut, for a few days of contemplation. On my first day there I was drawn to a small local beach. It was an overcast weekday in late August. There was only one other person there—a woman a few yards behind me. She was peering out over the water and looked in my direction. We were strangers, but it was one of those moments when it would seem rude not to acknowledge each other's presence.

"I hope I didn't disturb you, she said. "I just came here to think things out. Is that what you are doing?"

"Yes," I said, "exactly that."

She hesitated momentarily, looked at me pensively, and then began blurting out things, personal things, things that you sometimes can only tell a stranger, shielded with that relief of anonymity. She told me her husband had been unfaithful and was leaving her. She was middle-aged, getting divorced, diagnosed with breast cancer, and truly terrified. "I have to get a job. I don't know how to work, I don't know how to be a single mother, what if the car breaks down, who will fix it? How can I do everything by myself? I am afraid to be alone."

As she poured out her thoughts, I was startled by the fact that her fears sounded so familiar–that these exact same thoughts had filled my own head years before. I told her how I had been through so many of the same fears and I truly understood how much despair she felt. I told her I was the world's biggest coward, but I did get through it all, even cancer. She asked me all kinds of questions about how I handled *this,* and how I found out *that,* and even what did I do when my car broke down! She listened with great attention, as I recalled doing so many things on my own for the first time. Like her, I had gone straight from home to marriage and family, never having been alone.

She told me she thought I was just stronger than she but I told her I didn't believe that was the case. I just asked for help when I needed it and tried not to take on everything, all at once. I did what I could handle, a little bit each day, and eventually, I got through it.

She told me her name was Kelly and she said, "I know this may sound strange to you, and I hope you don't think I am crazy, but I was here praying for answers, and I think God sent you here to me." At that one moment so much became clear to me.

"No," I said, "You are here for me."

"How could I have possibly helped you?" she said. "All I did was tell you my troubles."

I told her how she made me remember all that I had survived, and how far I had come. I realized that all of those things were much worse than what I was facing now, so there was no reason to believe I couldn't pick myself up and get through this stuff, too.

Tears came to her eyes, and to mine, and we hugged each other spontaneously, then went our separate ways. I use that memory whenever a new challenge comes along, grateful for having met Kelly.

∂

My Moon Story

By Rachel Regenold

I was diagnosed with cancer one fall when I was a senior in college applying to law school. I was distraught but convinced myself that my illness and treatment would alter my life very little. For a time that was true because I was able to continue attending school full-time, working a part-time job, and applying for law school during chemotherapy.

I graduated from college the following spring, finishing chemotherapy not long afterwards. The initial good response to chemotherapy had slowed. At the appointment after my final round of chemo, I sat in the waiting area hoping to glimpse my doctor as he passed by. When he wouldn't meet my gaze, I knew the news wasn't good.

I broke down in tears when he said he wanted to do more tests and that I might need a bone marrow transplant.

My doctor firmly told me I would not be able to attend law school in the fall. I was a young woman with plenty of time for school, he said. But if I needed a bone marrow transplant, I would be in no condition to do that. I fell apart when I got home.

The worst was yet to come. I entered a two-month wait-and-see period. During those two months, not only my health, but my home and livelihood, were in flux. I had planned to move to Boston for law school in August, when the lease was up on my apartment, but now I was unsure where I would live. My job was contingent on my being a student, but I was no longer in school.

To make matters even worse, someone stole one of my credit cards and racked up charges over the limit. Then I was in a car accident that left me uninjured but having to negotiate the details of insurance and a car rental. My life was falling to pieces.

I was ragged with worry during those two months. One summer night I asked God for help. I begged for an end to the not-knowing. If I had to endure more treatment,

I would, but I could no longer stand not knowing what was next. I asked God to send me a sign.

The next night I was out running errands when I felt pulled onto the interstate. I enjoyed driving the 410 Loop around San Antonio. The hour-long drive to nowhere settled my mind as I made my way in a big circle around the city. The night sky was growing darker.

As I rounded a bend, something in the trees caught my eye. When I pulled clear of the trees, I saw the biggest, orange-est moon I had ever seen, full and hanging low in the sky. It took my breath away. The moment I saw it, I knew it was my sign from God: "Everything will be okay." Tears came to my eyes, but when I lost sight of the moon I lost faith. The moon came up every night. How could this be a sign from God?

A couple weeks later I had more tests, and my doctor gave me the all-clear—no more tests or treatment required, though I would have follow-up appointments for many years to come.

I have been in remission for twelve years now and no longer see an oncologist annually. Every time I see a full, orange moon hanging low in the sky, I remember God's message to me that "everything will be okay." And I have faith that it's true.

Dare to Trust

By Cathy AJ Hardy

it has been hard to say
    'i did what i could' ... when that means
        that i have to admit
          that i can't hold everything
            together
              all the time

to allow
  things
 to fall and crash and break
to allow
  things
  to get lost and not found
to allow misperceptions to be — without freaking
to allow

40

my carefully laid plans to

    fall apart

to allow

the feeling of emptiness

    to come close to me

        when i feel that things are slipping through my fingers

to allow my heart to say

    yes

      to You

in the midst of these moments

    and not lose heart

to be willing to be turned upside down

and shaken

    loose

      of my firm grip

        on

          things

so i can rest

    in my poverty

      and humanity

and dare to trust

      in your abundance

      and divinity

   and then celebrate the mystery

the paradox

  the miracle

of Emmanuel —

  God with us, God in us.

The Missing Puzzle Piece

By Angela Rae Clark

Journal Entry / May 20, 1996

My dream last night was of me as a little girl in the car
and angry about where we were going. I couldn't tell
anyone why, but I was terrified of visiting this place.

The scene changed: the little girl took my hand and
led me to a wall where a puzzle was hanging. It was a
puzzle that represented my life. All the events and people
I had experienced were in this picture. There was a
general, and familiar, sense of chaos—visible and
palpable—exactly how I felt during my waking hours. I
noted there was one piece missing in the lower right-hand
quadrant.

Then the girl motioned for me to lean over and
examine something in her hand as she strained to lift it
higher: It was a puzzle piece. Without saying a word she
expressed the importance of what was on that puzzle

piece. She was right, it was important. I looked in her eyes and nodded, acknowledging her wisdom and my understanding. Then she carefully placed it in the puzzle on the wall. In an instant the chaotic energy that had been overlaying the puzzle vanished. There was a thread from that piece to every person and event portrayed in the puzzle. My entire being resonated with relief and freedom with this piece of information.

The dream is crystal clear this morning—except what was on the single puzzle piece.

Journal Entry / December 25, 2010

Fourteen years of this dream and I finally know what is on the puzzle piece. The chaos in my life is gone, seemingly evaporated overnight. I am still, very still. There is an understanding of myself that I have been longing for my whole adult life. I now have memories that my brain chose to bury at the age of three. I don't know where these memories will take me, but my physical body is in a state of relief. I am acutely aware that my body has been spending enormous amounts of energy holding these memories inside. The freedom and liberation are immense.

Journal Entry / April 10, 2012

As each memory emerges, I experience a state of shock. I consciously navigate acceptance and integration of this new information into my story. Reliving the trauma is difficult. But I recognize that I cannot heal from that which I do not remember. How can I heal the wounds of rape if I can't acknowledge that it happened? Awareness and acceptance have been critical to navigating the storms of the past as I pick up and hold the broken debris. These relics lead me to a deeper understanding of myself. Healing and the ability to choose differently emerge from the brokenness.

I am continually amazed that everything I did before seeking professional help was exactly what the experts are guiding me through now, 17 months after the first memory emerged. I am grateful that I had such a connection to my innate wisdom. I have been guided efficiently through this journey. God has provided the people, resources and support that I needed at exactly the right moment—all I had to do was ask.

I believe that as we each commit to healing our wounds, whatever they are, that we create a healing ripple of energy into our immediate family and friends that spreads out over the Earth. I visualize that healing energy rippling out across the world frequently—some days it is what keeps me going. However, most days the ability to move forward and continue to heal comes from the inner freedom and healing that I have already experienced. The healed part of my soul reaches out to the wounded places and beckons me inside.

III.

MINDFULNESS

❧

~

Their Sidewalks

By Caroline A. Cataldo

From as early as I can remember, I have always loved cities. I would watch as the sea of suits rushed by me, wanting nothing more than to be one of those graceful women who would simultaneously add the click of their work heels and a one-sided telephone call to the soundtrack of urban life. I was just a kid and knew enough not to stare. Besides, a reciprocated smile would be out of the question. The lure of this world was very real, and I couldn't help but picture an older version of myself gliding down *their* sidewalk in my own pair of high heels.

That day finally came, and I became one of those women navigating public transportation to reach my internship in Boston's Theatre District. Old habits could not help but bubble up inside of me, and I caught myself staring straight into the face of corporate America. You know, it's funny. Although I walked in one of America's largest cities with hundreds of people pushing past me in rush hour traffic, I could not help but feel completely and utterly

alone.

I looked down at my feet. No, I was not wearing my little kid sneakers anymore. My feet were becoming blistered by heels. Didn't that make me one of those women I modeled my life after more than a decade ago? It was at that exact moment that a voice broke through my solitude:

Paper, Miss?

Uh, thanks.

You're very welcome, Miss. Now, you have a nice day.

Thanks so much.

You too.

With voices still ringing in my ears, I could not help but reciprocate the toothless smile of the weathered-looking *Metro* newspaper man that had just handed me a paper. That smile was the kind of human oneness that I had been craving from the people in a city that I claimed as my own.

I would continue to use the sidewalk of my "*Metro* man" for the remainder of the summer, making small conversation as he welcomed me to the city we both called home. I began to see things. No, not things…people. Each Thursday at the edge of Boston Common, "Man with the Red Baseball Hat" would be standing in his usual spot with tennis ball in hand, reading passages from the Bible. Every Tuesday and Wednesday, "Starbucks Guy" would be holding the coffee shop door, hoping for any spare change *his* customers might be willing to give him. Every day I searched for "my friends" through the crowds of bodies that littered the streets, wanting to know more about them but pausing just long enough to smile. Conversations were not always needed, but the brief moment of acknowledgment made them constants in my commute.

They say that what grabs your attention as a child gives you clues about who you are meant to be as an adult.

I guess I will never really know why I chose to start paying attention that summer. But I do know that this change in me sparked a chain reaction of self-understanding and direction that will shape the rest of my life. In the solitude of my city sidewalk commute, I found that the heels with which I am meant to tread these streets can never be disconnected from the worn-out sneakers of the *Metro* man. Now that I have seen them, I will always be drawn to the faces of the forgotten. Maybe that makes me different from most, but I think it is a kind of different that the world needs right now.

If I am not the one to pay attention, who else will?

The Crazy One

By Maddy Stella Fletcher

I kept this rose,

the one you bought for me,

out of the blue—

and I pressed it between the back pages of this book.

Its colour has faded, and its petals have become brittle,

like ancient paper, but I couldn't bear to throw it away —

the first flower ever given to me.

I trimmed it down and pressed it firmly,

until its thorns

left indentations in the page.

So now, even after I inevitably discard it —

shaking my head

or rolling my eyes

at the sentimentality of my youth,

I will still be able to turn to the back pages of this book

and find the thorny indentations there —
run my fingers over the tiny pock marks
and remember
that you once bought me a rose
out of the blue.

❧

Island Time

By Miyoko Hikiji

Summertime in the Midwest is tumultuous. The days that begin with warm sunrays that burn off morning dew, the air punctuated by the peeps of black-capped chickadees can turn to nights of ominous clouds and window rattling, nerve shattering thunder. In a single day, the weather can be calm, riotous, then quiet again, even calmer than it began.

Several family members and friends of mine have tried to rid themselves of these unpredictable storms by fleeing to the islands of Hawaii, if only for annual vacations. There is an allure that promises not only astronomical sunshine, but psychological warmth as well. For Midwesterners, these tropical islands are where the grass is truly greener.

My mother, an Iowan who moved to Hawaii for about five years, agrees that there's something special about "island time." Life seemed to move more slowly there, she reminisced, so it was easier to see what was important. Her attitude about Hawaii was simple: no worries.

My father took me back to Hawaii, to where he and my mother had lived, to show me the land, the lifestyle, the living they made there. And I could taste some of that appeal my mother had described, in the dripping sugar of a freshly cut pineapple and in the salty Pacific waves. I could feel it in the red dirt; I heard it from the strings of a ukulele. For a short time, I also was transfixed by "island time." But I, too, returned home.

Recently I planned a getaway to Washington Island as a weekend antidote to a frenetic work schedule. This 23-square-mile island, seven miles off the peninsula of Wisconsin, can only be accessed by ferry. As I stepped out of my car and onto the deck, I felt a sudden stillness. I watched seagulls, nesting along the rocky banks, get further and further away and the calm, cold waters of Lake Michigan in the east and Green Bay in the west engulf me. I was safely afloat in contemplation and quiet: no worries.

The island has a sparse population, around 600, and one main road that snakes along the island's periphery, interrupted only by a single flashing red stoplight. Before finding my inn, I found a pub where the locals filled me in on what life was like while filling me up on beer grown from the island's wheat. They spoke easily, as if we'd been longtime friends, and I was certain that if I had not mentioned I had reservations at the inn, one of them would have invited me to stay in her guest room. To my surprise, "island time" also existed on a not-so-tropical island. No palms, no waterfalls, no worries.

I spent the following day touring some homes and the evening walking at the water's edge. I watched the sun extinguish into the bay, feeling content but absolutely alone, my own island, disconnected from the mainland and altogether homeless.

It was then I realized that I could find "island time" on Washington Island, or the Hawaiian Islands, or any place at all, in fact, if first I placed the "island spirit" within me. That spirit was the choice to embrace all of life: flood or drought, sand or rock, sweet or bitter, while reaching or falling or dancing, until dying.

I brought the map from Washington Island home and placed it at the edge of my desk. I didn't need to reference it there; it does serve a purpose here. Navigating the paths of my own life is tricky. I have encountered more than one stoplight, dozens of yield signs, a few falling rocks, scenic views and two dead ends. So when I need island time and cannot jet away to a resort, the map sits to remind me of the island spirit I discovered in Wisconsin. Like summer, life is tumultuous, a constant exchange of harmony for discord and the calm after the storm; the peace in the end—no worries—is eternal.

ॐ

The Filter Queen

By Becca Briscoe (aka Peanut Beranski)

"Most people are about as happy
as they make up their minds to be."
—Abraham Lincoln

I took my 2003 Ford Fungus in to have an oil change last week at Jiffy Lube. The attendant asked if I wanted the premium oil filter or just the regular one. He posed the question in such a tone that if I had answered the "regular one," I would have been guilty of car abuse.

"I'll take the premium, of course," I said. "Only the BEST for the Fungus."

Each time I go through this ritual, it annoys me. If I had a garage, I could easily change my own oil and filter. I learned the skill when I owned a marina and could only afford a mechanic on a part-time basis. Inboard/outboard boat motors are car engines with propellers attached instead of tires. I changed the oil in many, many boats over the course of ten years. In fact, I would consider myself an expert at changing oil filters.

I also learned how to change the filter in my furnace, my water purifier, my nebulizer and my fish tank. I have changed a swimming pool filter, a filter in the Wet Vac and my home oxygen condenser. I suppose you could call me a Filter Queen.

But the most important filter I ever learned to change is the one directly connected to my brain. Like any other filter, its purpose is to prevent unwanted material from passing through and taking root deep in my mind.

In 1993, while on a Christian Women's Retreat, God let me know that I needed to change the filter of my thoughts. I have always had a good sense of humor, but for many years, I used humor to keep people where I wanted them—at arm's length. In a moment of enlightenment, God convinced me that He had not given me the gift of a quick wit so that I could hide from people or control them; He gave the gift to bring people into a closer relationship with Him.

That August night, I decided to let God's Grace be the filter through which I would process incoming information. This personal cosmic shift did not prevent bad news from being broadcast on CNN or hurtful gossip from spreading around the office. People still get snarky while waiting in line at the grocery, and horns still blare when I fail to stomp on the gas pedal within one second of the light changing to green. Prices of everything continue to rise, resources continue to dwindle, and the doctor still says I need a pacemaker.

This God Filter allows me to react in a more positive way to negative input. It is possible to choose joy over misery, to concentrate on beautiful objects and good friends instead of giving any energy over to whiners and naysayers.

I cherish my God Filter, and I continually check it to make sure it is not clogged with stinky stuff. I still see the funny side of things, but God showed me how best to react to life so that more people will come to know His unending Love and Grace.

As if my God Filter weren't enough, God gave me another gift that hot summer night in 1993 when he said nine words that gave me a new perspective:

"Peanut," He said, "life is too short to stuff a mushroom."

❧

Love More Fiercely

By Barbara Knight Katz

Radiation zaps my tattooed flesh
while music from "Titanic" fills the room.
I pretend that I am not afraid.

I will love more people now
and love the ones I love more fiercely.
I will memorize their faces.

I will pay close attention
to gray juncos hopping near the door
on sun-drenched mornings.

I will lie down on new-mown grass,
breathe in the pungent earthy scent
of long summer afternoons.

I will consult myself, oak trees
and the moon's reflections on the lake
on all important matters.

I will step out when I die,
tentative at first, past the edge
of familiar grounding.

I will ride on ocean waves
farther and farther out, tasting
salt of the full tide.

ॐ

Finding Home in Holland Park

By SuzAnne C. Cole

The parks of London are justly famous, for each has its own flavor. In St. James's Park, birds peck treats from the hands of tourists and statesman alike. Further afield, one can ramble through the vast expanses of Hampstead Heath and dream of Bronte novels or explore the magnificent botanical collections of Kew Gardens. However, my favorite London park is Holland Park, located just west of Kensington Park. For one glorious year we lived in a townhouse three blocks from this park, where I walked every day.

In the early 17th century Holland Park and its stately manor, Holland House, were part of the estate of the Earl of Holland. World War II bombing destroyed the house, and in 1952 the London County Council bought the estate, the last private one remaining in London. Parts of the house were restored—the east wing became a youth hostel, the central section an open-air theatre, the ballroom an expensive restaurant, the orangery and icehouse, art galleries.

Besides these attractions, the park also contains the Commonwealth Institute museum; tennis courts, football pitch and cricket field; squash courts; iris, rose, and Japanese gardens; children's play park; and my favorite area, 28 acres of natural woodlands, "the Wildernesse" of the original estate. Here gravel paths meander through woods of oaks, birches, limes, chestnuts, cedars and rhododendrons; naturalized daffodils, bluebells, and crocuses make a splendid display in the spring. Peafowls and guinea fowls parade, rabbits and squirrels hurry past on unidentified errands, and birds including woodpeckers, ring-neck doves, English robins, and mallards go about their business.

After we moved into our home, I ran in the park for exercise as soon as the gates were unlocked in the early morning. Later in the day I strolled through the park, letting its peaceful beauty help me recover from the stress preceding the move, when I taught six college classes, co-authored a textbook, sold a house, and helped one son choose a college and another adapt to the idea of a new school in his senior year, all without my husband, who moved nine months before we did.

I learned, like the English, to appreciate sunny days. Walking through the park on warm, clear days, I saw children enjoying the sun on their nude bodies, shirtless men stretched out napping, and women on lunch breaks removing stiff white shirts—and sometimes their dark skirts as well—for a few minutes of sun.

For two pounds per annum ($3.50/year), I became a Friend of Holland Park, which entitled me, once a month, to walk through areas normally fenced off from visitors. During one walk our guide pointed out a den. Two miles from the Marble Arch, four blocks from Indian takeaways and a tube station, a fox had made himself at home, living off the young, slow and weak among the park's animal and bird population.

Sometimes I picnicked on sandwiches in the park or had soup in the small cafeteria in the youth hostel. And when we had to leave London, a friend treated me to a farewell lunch in the Belvedere Restaurant there. We sat by an open window, a scarlet, orange, and golden rose garden glowing just beyond its frame, both sharpening and relieving my sadness at leaving this glorious park.

Last spring, on a return visit to London, I left my downtown hotel early one morning. With nowhere I had to be and nothing I had to do until 5:00 that evening, I headed west to Holland Park, heading home.

ॐ

Paint Color—Cracked Wheat

By Lori Ulrich

Our 20-year-old bathroom is in great need
of a makeover, paint peels, there are
scars, the walls breathe life's nicks.
Cobwebs hang from the ceiling, sun shines
on complex patterns. Winter's brightness
is merciless, shows dust spread across lights,
wall stains.

My son is traveling.
He paints with a brush of color, murals
of Mexico, ceiling to floor, through rural
countrysides, drug-cartel cities, lazy surf
towns and bars, leaves his prints
on the hearts of the people he meets.

I wash, scrub, scrape hard crust off linoleum,
push harder than I need to, prep for painting.
I tape the parts we don't want paint on.
I start with the trim, edge ceilings, floors with
a brush, each stroke changes light green
to cracked wheat, a light golden color
suited to our country home.
The roller brush glides up and down, back
and forth, covers past stories.

I paint my son into memories. Optimistic, I
thought a fresh coat of paint, some new
pictures, a new shower curtain and
shaggy-haired beige rugs would do it.
I could paint my way into forgetting
he is not here.

IV.

RESILIENCE

ॐ

ॐ

Learning to Trust My Legs

By Valerie D. Benko

The summer sun warmed my skin as I strolled down the sidewalk thinking about the playground dedication ceremony I was on my way to attend. Seconds later I was face down, staring at the gray concrete, stunned.

After sitting up, a cursory inspection of the sidewalk revealed that it was new. There wasn't a slope or a bump. I didn't trip, stumble, twist my ankle or even brace myself because there was no warning that a fall was coming.

Beautiful yellow sunflowers arranged in neat pots stood tall on lengthy green stalks near where I had fallen, partially concealing me from on-lookers. A sigh escaped with the realization that I did need to get up. My right leg was numb from a multiple sclerosis flare up, but my foot was fine. A quick inspection found no cuts or scrapes. Then it occurred to me why I had fallen.

In the two years since my autoimmune disease diagnosis, which affects the central nervous system, stories were told from others with the disability about how their legs had given out without warning. My first MS fall had just occurred!

Two of my colleagues, who had been waiting for me in the car, were hurrying over. Concern laced their faces. Fighting back tears, I told them I was fine, got to my feet and smoothed my skirt. My right leg was much weaker, but I could walk.

The ride to the dedication ceremony felt impossibly long as the feeling of defeat set in. I kept up the lie that I was fine, but I wasn't. Since starting treatment, there haven't been any serious problems with my MS. My career sprung in a new direction with a position in Community Relations, where attendance at events such as press conferences, award dinners, groundbreaking ceremonies and other community outreach initiatives is expected. This position requires me to be at the top of my game. Not falling down on sidewalks.

The gentleman speaking at the playground dedication advised those in attendance to gather on the wood chips surrounding the playground for the ribbon cutting and pictures. I didn't trust my leg. What if it betrayed me again? Reluctantly, I stepped onto the wood chips to hold the ribbon and smiled a fake smile for the camera.

The fear of falling haunted me the rest of the day, crawling deep into my psyche and filling every thought. Real concerns surfaced. I cross streets every day to get to work. What if I fall in front of a vehicle? Back at the office, that fear tethered me to my desk. Documents would have to wait to be printed; the risk of falling in the hallway was too great.

At the end of the day, as I was preparing to shut down my computer, it made a "ding," signaling a message had arrived. It was a work e-mail from another colleague who was known for putting a cast of rotating inspirational quotes as her signature. The content of the e-mail could wait until the next day for a response, but a quick scan for her quote made me catch my breath. "Don't be the girl that fell. Be the girl that got back up." It was attributed to Jenette Stanley.

The quote stuck with me on the drive home. I could live every day of my life in fear that I may fall again, even if I never fall. Or I could let go of the fear and choose to get back up and continue on my journey. I chose the latter.

ॐ

Opening Up

By Diane Glass

People describe me as "poised under pressure." Few know this poise masked a disability, family secrecy and terror. Born in 1947 with an open spine—spina bifida—I was predicted to die within days. When I was still alive at ten months, the University of Iowa Hospitals closed my spine and sent me home. As I grew up, no one talked with me about my condition, and I was cautioned not to talk to anyone else.

Yet problems plagued me. An impaired bladder leaked without warning, but emptied only with a catheter wielded by my parents. A tethered spinal cord caused severe leg pain as I grew. A sense of shame shrouded my heart.

Going to school meant figuring things out on my own. When other girls went to the bathroom during breaks in elementary school, I went too, stayed in the stall and hoped no one would notice the lack of tinkling. Then I dashed home at lunch to be secretly catheterized.

One fateful day in junior high, during a stressful test, my bladder completely emptied. I pretended not to notice the urine leaking around my chair. At the end of the class, skirt dripping, I walked out the door, dashed across an open field and through the back door of our house. Within minutes I was sobbing, curled up on my bed.

"Grandma prays for you," my mother said, clearly distressed. My second-grade class picture tucked into the pages of Grandma's Ukrainian Bible did little to comfort me.

"Our choral concert is tonight at school," I wept. "I have to go back. But how can I face everyone?" There was no answer. Hours later, I dressed for the concert and returned to school, alone, to sing, then go home and try to forget the humiliating exposure of the day.

"There's Betsy Wetsy," one of my classmates teased. I forced a smile and strode out the room.

Years passed with few knowing about my disability, covered as it was by a carefully constructed yet fragile grace. At age 52, this composure was shattered when a diagnosis of breast cancer opened me to the world of cards and flowers, phone calls—and questions.

Will you have a mastectomy? A lumpectomy? What about the other breast? What stage is your cancer? What is it like to possibly face death?

The questions startled me. At a breast cancer support group meeting, the leader introduced herself by giving us her name and telling us she had had a mastectomy. The introductions continued around the table—some mastectomies, some lumpectomies. Horrified as my turn came, I mumbled something about having had surgery and waiting for chemotherapy.

As the weeks progressed, my discomfort subsided; it was okay to open up and talk about breast cancer. Runs, walks, pink ribbons, t-shirts and survivor celebrations normalized this unfortunate disease. Sharing with friends gave me a sense of wholeness.

Yet my soul felt betrayed. If I could talk about my breasts, why couldn't I talk about my bladder?

Millions of people in this country suffer from incontinence, often in isolation and loneliness. Even more people suffer from the burden of secrecy about other conditions.

Poise and composure helped me get this far, and for that I am grateful. Now my priority is to honor my whole body and the life we've shared together. Yet I struggle with the questions. When to talk? What to say? And to whom?

One thing is certain. I don't want to die not having healed from unrevealed secrets. And I don't want whatever wisdom is uncovered by my life story to die with me.

❧

This Abundance Is Mine!

By Deborah Jansen

Curly stands of blue-green kale anchor my garden. Arugula and chives claim a spot near the path. Swiss chard veined with ruby, orange and white grows in center stage. I blend rainbow salads, colorful stir-fry and vegetable lasagna. Dreams of garden-to-table abundance are on my mind.

However, a reality check shows another source of abundance. Aphids, spider mites, and cabbage moths are on the loose. Beetle larvae emerge from the soil. I'm disgusted with these creatures who've invaded *my* territory. I discover I've claimed abundance as *my possession* again—something I claim and defend.

A master gardener tells me, "We're the only creatures in nature who can look around and learn from what we see. We can adjust our environment, but that doesn't make it ours." He tilts his straw hat and adds, "What is nature trying to show you? What does the garden need?"

Hmmm. Today, I return to the garden to pull Swiss chard that's dotted with moth eggs. I trowel the dirt, blend in organic insect repellant and plant zucchini instead. I unfold a sheer cloth, shake it into the wind and let it fall like a veil over the row. The cover keeps cabbage moths away while allowing sunlight to shine through. I pour water into the birdbath so robins will come for a drink and stay for a larvae snack. I yank out flowering cilantro and dill, but leave some to attract wasps, who might feed on aphids.

"When a student is ready, a teacher will appear," the Zen proverb goes. The "teacher" referred to in this saying might be a person, but it could just as well be anything that shifts someone's focus. I'm not especially talented at gardening, but one of my consistent teachers is the garden. It teaches me the dance of release over and over again.

Perhaps another teacher—and I resist admitting it—is the cabbage moth. That insect shows me when I'm clinging and fighting—not just in the literal sense, but also in a spiritual, emotional sense. In a garden, it's delightful to plan, arrange and set the stage for abundance. All too often, I cling to that plan—even feel entitled to it. But the appearance of the cabbage moth teaches me to return to a path of wisdom—accept reality as it is, not as I would have it. Embrace the courage to change what I can. Celebrate the abundance that is already here. Be present in the now.

❧

Page Turners

By Lori Ulrich

My daughter and I meet in the bruised pages,
between readings,
words we clung to, can't let go of

words we wrote in permanent pen
punctuate the ends of our sentences, finalize,
pages are worn, repeated readings of our story
smear the white paper, smudged fingerprints
bend the corners, carry memory

pink eraser marks rub where
inked phrases failed to dissipate
the words *"I am sorry."*
blend in with transcribed trials of words
crossed out, elusive epistle

we bandage wounded words
scars recognized
we meet on clean paper
thin blue lines we write on
part our pages
continue to write our story

I am signed by her,
her name reiterates itself,
within the written pages
ink flows with long hugs,
bodies bruised by pressing too hard
against the book we won't close

Hair Story

By Michelle Foster

Long hair has always been a part of me. I grew up pulling it back into a blondish ponytail before riding, feeling the ecstasy that young girls feel when they act, just a little, like their horse. In college it was wild. Later, traveling through Asia, it grew as long as my journey. I loved to feel it catch the wind, to feel the air as part of me.

My hair reached the top of my thighs when I was diagnosed with cancer. Before I began chemo, I dressed in a newly loose suit, and John photographed my hair. I went to a stylist who washed it carefully, braided the thickest part and sliced it off. What was left was very cute: lighter, it sprung up and curled and waved.

My mother came with me, and afterward we went to wig shops. We wondered: why are wig shops always on forsaken downtown streets? Why do they put purple wigs in the windows?

We stretched and pulled and tugged on hairpieces and, although shop attendants "blended" my own hair in around the edges, nothing I could afford looked natural.

We finally found one—or maybe just gave in—and I wore it to John's office. He talked for a while and admired my new haircut, and only after an hour or so he said: "Weren't you going to go wig shopping today?" and said he couldn't tell the wig wasn't my own hair and kissed my head.

A few weeks later, as summer faded into autumn and my treatments progressed, my hair was still intact; it literally hung in there.

"I am so glad," John said one cool night, nuzzling me, "that your hair isn't falling out. That wig made you look like a 1950s suburban housewife."

Within a few days, it fell out in chunks. It left trails in the house. It flew off in fall winds. It clogged drains, and I feared for the engine on the hand-me-down vacuum. We cut it shorter, but it was like the leaves—after a while, there was almost nothing left, and we settled into winter.

But I never did put on that wig. One early spring day, peach fuzz started growing back in, soft and downy and fresh. And it stayed.

❧

Thank You, Dr. Seuss

By Tasneem Damji

The evening routine in our household can go one of two ways. My four-year old son can eat his dinner, have a bath, brush his teeth, put on his pajamas and get into bed with no fuss. Or he can turn into Mr. Negotiator Extraordinaire, bargaining for (and usually winning) longer time in the bath, doing everything possible to procrastinate going to bed—from requesting water to needing to check something in the living room and convincing me that he *has* to wait up for his dad who is working late.

Eventually, we snuggle next to each other, get under the covers and turn on his flashlight. It is story time, my favorite time of the day, when we are both relaxed and focused on the book we're about to read. And for the next fifteen minutes or so, I forget about the stressful day at work, the dishes piling up in the sink or the broken light bulb.

Tonight's story: *Oh, the Places You'll Go* by Dr. Seuss. It was gifted to me by a friend before we moved to Tajikistan, where my husband is from. This move came after a number of conversations, *bang-ups* and *hang-ups* (as Dr. Seuss says happens to everyone during their lives) and reflection on how to live an authentic life. It was my deep desire to expose my son to his family on the other side of the world, live a simple life and make it possible for him to immerse himself in a new culture.

I didn't want to be like those people in the book waiting for *Another Chance*—this was our chance and I was not going to let it pass. It was not an easy move— leaving a secure job at the local university, moving away from family and friends and all the comforts in life. It became harder as I began to tell more people.

While there were many supporters, it was difficult to hear people questioning my motivations and telling me how I would be doing a disservice to my son by taking him to a "poor" country. What kept me going strong during this emotionally draining time was a phone conversation I had a couple of months after deciding to move.

The woman on the phone longed to go work in Bangladesh, where her father's family was from. She had never been there and felt like something was missing.

I got off the phone and smiled—I knew in my heart that our move was the right thing to do and that it was up to me, my son's mother, to never have my son ache in this way.

We've been living in Tajikistan for almost six months, and my son is showing me why we made this move. He loves spending time with his family—making traditional dumplings with his grandmother, looking at his grandfather's rock collection, kicking a ball with his uncle and running around the house with his cousin. He goes to preschool and speaks Russian fluently for his age and loves going on the school bus with his friends.

Tonight, when I finish reading the book, I turn to my son and tell him that it's important to do what your heart tells you, even if others don't agree with you. As Dr.

Seuss says, "*Remember that Life's a Great Balancing Act. Just never forget to be dexterous and deft. And never mix up your right foot with your left.*"

He smiles at me and closes his eyes.

❧

Twenty Push-Ups

By Stacia Duvall

There is a modern-day fairytale that begins like this:

Once upon a time in the midst of raising children, a lovely lady who had grown a bit complacent was surprised one day when her mate of many years said, "I don't love you anymore." When the last child went off to college, he was with someone who made him feel younger, and she was alone.

It was the first time she had lived alone. She ate cereal for dinner on occasion. She let the house get messy. She played her kind of music—and loudly. She slept in the middle of her king-sized bed. She chose when and where and why and how without consulting anyone.

In the quiet of that empty nest she remembered being 22. She could not recall exactly why she thought he was the one. She could recollect that when college ended and careers began, marriage seemed like the next logical step. She remembered being caught up in a gale of love that had swept in on the wind of fear. Everyone was being selected, one by one. Would she be the person nobody picked?

And suddenly, years later, it had happened. She was not picked, and now she was alone.

This was not what she expected when she was young and raising her family and being supportive and living on the assumption that the future would be spent with the person to whom she had vowed her forever.

After time spent wallowing, she decided one day to call upon her remaining strength. She decided that from now on, she needed to do a couple of push-ups and try something new each day. Before long, she could do twenty push-ups, and she had traveled by herself to a place a thousand miles away.

She found herself doing many things she had never done before, like asking for help and making people worry and undoing another button on her blouse. She felt amazingly strong.

After some time, she started liking the idea of spending the rest of her life with a person she had recently come to know.

Herself.

One day, after she realized that how she felt about herself could be called love, a handsome man rode in and tried to "woo" her. He tried and tried, but she doubted there was space in herself to love another now that she so loved herself. She was afraid she might go back to where she had been when she was left by her husband.

But the handsome man was patient. He treated her with kindness and consideration unlike anything she had known before, which caused her to consider him differently. She could see in him quality and value. And she noticed that she smiled more and that her eyes seemed brighter when they were together.

One day as they danced, she told him she loved him. The words popped from her mouth before she had time to think of their meaning. And she knew for a fact there was space in herself to love another.

And the amazingly strong woman could see that whatever way the wind blew and whichever moment of the far-off future she was in, she would not be afraid. For she loved herself.

So she vowed that from that day forward she would be true and loving and faithful.

To herself.

And she felt happy, content and at peace with that prospect.

ॐ

Winds of Change

By Sharon Meixsell

The wind blows fiercely
My hair whips around my face
I brush it away from my eyes
It is not cold

I look around me
The trees bending
The leaves waving
The sun shining

I say to the trees,
"Don't worry, you are safe,
for your roots keep you planted.
You belong to something greater."

To the leaves

I say, "Be brave, for soon you

will be going on an adventure.

You will travel many places before you die.

This is your time to get ready.

Ready for the unknown

And all of the glorious possibilities

Which lie ahead."

❧

Summer Drive

By Kathleen Adams

In my first year as a new driver, I'd had some mishaps with the car. A high pop fly at a baseball game bounced off the roof of my dad's car, leaving a dent. Soon I was driving a used Ford Fairlane with a broken fuel gauge, and more than once I ran out of gas. Then one foggy night I backed right into a tree. Today, however, was sunny and dry.

"Laurie," I said to my sister," Let's go shopping. "

Our dad didn't understand the point of leaving the farm without a well-defined purpose, but Mom appreciated our need to explore the wider world and she gave the OK. Laurie and I headed to DeKalb. I was dabbling with the idea of frosting my mousy blond hair. Convincing Dad would be the hard part. As I studied color options at the Rexall Drug, I pondered the best way to persuade him.

On the trip home Laurie, looked at the new *Seventeen* magazine while I drove. As I sped along an open stretch of highway, a driver coming from the opposite direction was passing on a hill. Cresting that hill, my Ford Fairlane was nose to nose with his full-size cement truck. Was the truck driver's shocked expression a reflection of my own panic?

"Ahhhhhh!!!" I shrieked.

Automatically I swerved to the right, just missing a head on collision. Time slowed as we lurched through tall, thick ditch weeds toward a thin metal culvert post. I pressed my full weight against the brake pedal. I squeezed the blood from my fingers against the steering wheel. I screamed to myself, *No! Don't hit it!* But there was nothing I could do. *I've done it again. Dad will be disappointed.* At last I heard the crunch of metal against post.

Trembling and teary, I crawled out of the car. Two other cars—cars I had no awareness of—had also gone into the ditch. The cement truck did not stop. The driver of the car behind us, a middle-aged man, kept saying, "You did just the right thing. You saved our lives."

People gathered. Police came. I couldn't stop shaking.

We sat in the back seat of the police car to give the official account of the accident. I was too stunned to say much and began to worry. *How will Laurie and I get home? What should we do with the car? How will I tell Dad?* Then, to my surprise, I glanced up to see my father's face peering through the car window. He was driving to DeKalb when he noticed a car like mine in the ditch.

That evening, Uncle Gertis and Aunt Edith joined us for supper. As I told about the accident, I could see my Dad's beaming face. Everyone applauded my actions.

I didn't know what to make of the day's events.

How did that steering wheel get turned? Did God himself intervene? Do I have a guardian angel who was on her toes that day? Or, is it OK to take credit for what happened? After all, those were my hands on the steering wheel.

I still don't know the answers to these questions. But I live my life knowing that:

Life is fragile, so live each day with purpose and joy.

Unseen forces surround and support you. You need not fear.

Stay in touch with what you think, feel and love so that when you need to call quickly on your inner resources you'll be ready to respond.

Like a quiet summer day that surprises us with a storm, this ordinary day suddenly became a life-defining one. In a single moment everything had changed.

V.

B E A U T Y

༄

.

❧

Living on the Ridge:
The Clothesline

By Patricia Ambrose Griffin

Welcome to the Ridge, one of a gazillion knobs protruding from Earth in Garrard County, Kentucky, where bobcats still roam.

The latest bend in the road of life transports me at the end of summer to this beautiful region, where I am staying until winter. Living on a ridge means lots of sunshine and wind. Hence, the first item of business is putting up a clothesline.

Today is a very good day to hang clothes outside. There is a pleasant breeze, the sun is shining and the temperature is just right.

In my enthusiasm to use my clothesline, hung and knotted tightly by my brother, I recall our mother wiping hers clean with a damp cloth before each use. The memory evokes a smile and touches my heart.

The smell of the fresh outdoors lingers in the clothes. No fabric softener can match it. And I love the crispness of the garments, dried by energy-efficient nature.

As a teenager I was given the chore of ironing the flat pieces like handkerchiefs and pillow slips. Mom would sprinkle water on the air-dried garments, then roll them up tight and save them in the fridge for ironing day. As I unrolled and ironed each piece, the fresh smell immediately returned to my nostrils.

As a child my job was to hand my mother clothespins as she hung the wash. I would wait for her to shake the wet garment with vigor, listening to the crack of each shake and imagining each wrinkle biting the dust.

In my enthusiasm to help her, I'd hand her too many clothespins, but she never admonished me for my generosity. Instead, she'd put the extra pins in her mouth, awaiting the next garment.

In those days most clothespins weren't the powerful spring-loaded type. Rather, they were perfectly straight wood with a split down the middle that naturally expanded to hold the cloth. They had a nicely carved wooden cap on top that looked like a beret. The head fit nicely in my mother's mouth.

Sometime later, she started using the spring-loaded pins; that's when I'd amuse myself by putting one on each of my fingertips and pretend that I had long fingernails. I'd go around touching the trees and bushes, trying to pick up something to no avail because my "fingernails" got in the way.

It didn't take long before the tight clothespin-fingernails started hurting and I'd have to remove them. That's when I'd watch in wonder as the pink returned to my bloodless fingertips.

Later in the day Ma would check the laundry for dampness. She'd busily rearrange the pieces that were damp, rotating them so the air would finish drying those areas. Often she'd have to find a new sunny spot for them to dry.

At the end of our washday my assistance was again required. My duty was to collect the clothespins and to check the ground for any stray pins that may have popped off when the wind blew too hard. Mother was frugal with her clothespins. Sometimes she'd pin two pieces together at both ends. So I knew how important these pins were to her.

Recompense for my hard labor? You bet! I received boatloads of fresh air and sunshine and became Mom's best helper!

These precious memories accompany me on my first hanging of the wash on the ridge.

My Reverie

By Jean Naviaux

"I'd stay if you'd do what I tell you to do," I said to my mother when I was about five.

She'd just sent my neighbor friend home—against my wishes, of course. (I always remember it as being because the little girl had struck my forehead with a rock and made it bleed, but that doesn't ring true, does it?)

Anyway, whatever the reason, I'd decided to run away from home.

Mom came up to my bedroom to help me pack some clothes and my stuffed animals and, when I decided to take my baby brother with me, some diapers. She sat on the suitcase to make it easier to close, and she carried it downstairs for me because it was so heavy.

Once we got through the screen door and out onto the front porch, I changed my mind.

As a kid, I loved books about children who left home and lived off the "fatta the land." My favorite, by A H Seaman, told the tale of some boys and girls who survived on an island—with a cave and some bad guys—until they were rescued.

I also enjoyed *The Adventures of Huckleberry Finn* (although I hated the King and the Duke) and *My Side of the Mountain*. Huck rafted down the Mississippi, and Sam Gribley lived in a hollowed-out tree in the Catskills. Huck "borrowed" his food and Sam ate "wild greens" and game. I figured if I ran away from home, I could manage on dandelion greens, berries, and fish.

Well that was then: I'm a half century older now and I've yet to get away. I want to distance myself, if just for a little while, from Miami—the panhandler with no nose, television, rude and judgmental people, traffic, abandoned cats and smushed ducks, palm trees, face-eating monsters, maggots, heat and humidity, traffic, golf, people who delude themselves, politics, dirty underwear and people in general.

"I want the sky at midnight, the mountains at noon." A little cabin in the woods would be nice, with a stone fireplace, a comfy bed and eleven pillows. I'd stock my kitchen with coffee, Chardonnay, breads, cheeses and salad vegetables. Then I'd lunch on the porch, breathing in the cool fresh air and surrendering to the silence.

My reverie has whisked me to the here and now, so I settle in, and by midafternoon I'm ready to explore. I meander for miles along a vaguely familiar trail, not sure where I'm going but not really minding either; the lack of direction is comforting.

On my left, a stream follows the path and invites me to visit. When I kneel to touch its waters, I see black minnows darting here and there, and I flip a stone with a stick to check for crawdaddies. "Still there," I think to myself.

Around the bend and an hour or so later, I chance upon a tiny meadow sprinkled with wildflowers. I leave the path to sit for a while, plucking violets, making chains, encircling them about my neck and wrists. "There's more ahead," I realize. "I've caught glimpses—a waterfall, mountain peaks and a blue, blue sky."

But for now, I lie down to rest. The leaves of the tall trees above and the grasses and mosses below envelop me in a warm green blanket. I recall an old '40s song my mother often sang to lull me to sleep: "There's a long, long trail a-winding into the land of my dreams, where the nightingales are singing and a white moon beams."

Sensing her presence, I close my eyes.

ॐ

Stone and Oak

By Barbara Knight Katz

All morning I have been looking
for a word to tell you what I feel
inside this smooth white stone
resting on my palm, what it is like
to see the arching stretch of willow oak,
its arms covered in green sunshine,
while I swing slowly in my hammock,
but all I can tell you is that the beauty
that is in the stone and in the oak
meets something inside me
as if it strikes a tuning fork
and a low throbbing pain
or joy vibrates and all
the particles of my world
curve and flow into one wave.

❧

The Heavy House

By Becca Briscoe (aka Peanut Beranski)

"Please…please, I don't want to go." I begged my mother
as I tried to escape.

"You're going…now get in the car—don't make me
count."

In bitter resignation, I took my seat in the middle of
the backseat in our Chevy Bel Air. My older brother was
on my left and younger sister on my right. *Am I forever
destined to ride the hump?* I thought as we started our bi-
monthly pilgrimage to Oloney Street in Indianapolis, my
father's childhood home.

My grandparents' bungalow sat mid-block on a
narrow city street northeast of the business district. It
offered very few amenities for the energy level of a four-
year old. One exception was a large, well-groomed
municipal park a block to the north that had numerous
swingsets, a massive central pavilion and a public

swimming pool. I was forbidden to go there without adult supervision, but I remember sitting on the front porch swing jealously watching other kids play and swim. At the opposite end of the street was a Rexall Drug Store. The windows covered in brightly painted signs promoted everything from cologne to Carter's Little Liver Pills. I often wondered if I had a little liver because I was a kid.

I called the Oloney Street home the "Heavy House" because everything about it was intense and gloomy. The doors were weathered old wood, the floors were clad with musty green wool carpet, there was grey-flocked wallpaper and curtains that were saturated with the smell of my grandfather's cigar smoke.

Even the conversations at dinner were heavy. Grandpa would tell my dad and brother about the importance of setting goals and having responsibilities while my mother listened patiently to lectures on child rearing and good hygiene.

The only light in the Heavy House was my great grandmother, Mammer. She was a loving, petite woman who wore hearing aids. In the 1950s, hearing aids were the sizes of two decks of cards. Mammer wore her aids around her neck with wires that led up to cumbersome and uncomfortable earpieces.

"You know, Peanut, your Grandpa made me go deaf with all his bellowing and cursing. That's why when he talks, I just turn off my magic ears."

"But, Mammer, if your ears are off, how can you hear me?"

"I can always hear you, Peanut, because you speak straight to my heart," she said as she patted the box resting on her chest.

ॐ

Soul's Shimmer

By Angela Renkoski

I have always been drawn to the shimmering reflection of sunlight upon water, the glorious sparkling ripples blended into a harmonious dance of beauty. It's not unique to summer, but I easily see the surge of the season's bounty in shimmer's abundant allure and artistry. I also am a summer baby, a Leo born on the 18th of August, who craves basking in the sun as must lions soaking up rays on the African plains.

I estimate hundreds of shimmers on surfaces of rivers, lakes, seas and fountains have caught my eye and breath through the years. In St. Louis, where I lived a year ago, a pond in my neighborhood park cast a sparkly shimmer, its dappled surface often ruffled by ducks and swans as they paddled about. Now in Los Angeles and finishing a graduate program in spiritual psychology, the long shimmer stretching on the ocean's horizon to infinity beckons me to pay homage and renew our connection. For, in this time of extreme spiritual growth, as I search for my purpose and shed the detritus of limiting beliefs that no longer serve me, it is the shimmer that brings me home to myself, wherever my body happens to be.

I have adopted the shimmer as a personal symbol and integrated it into an affirmation around the quality of trust I am growing—trust in myself, trust in Spirit, trust in the world as good. Its beauty is one thing, its blending of disparate particles of light and water against the background of an infinite sky another. Even on cloudy days when the reflection is smaller or a bit dimmer, I can trust the Light is always there. I also remind myself how it sometimes takes a certain angle of viewing the water for the shimmer to be visible, and I am applying that idea to the effort of finding work, improving relationships, dealing with losses—the challenge just needs a new perspective for its benefit to shine forth.

The memory, the imprint, of Light upon my soul leads me to a deeper truth. In the shimmer, beneath the surface, beneath the individual drops of water and rays of light, lies a divine pattern uniting the froth of my life into a whole. I stand before the water and feel compelled to cast my disparate thoughts, cares and illusions of "not enough" onto the water's depths. Time and again, what the ego sees as dross joins with the sparkles. As it is breathtakingly transformed into radiance, my heart is pulled into the Oneness of pure beauty, peace and love. My edges soften, my mind yields and I am whole.

These qualities inspire me to state my affirmation this way: "I am trusting in the shimmer of the Divine Presence within me. It illumines my thoughts and guides my footsteps, and I am giving and receiving the warmth of its love." Drawn inward to the truth of my being, I instantly recognize that beautiful Light and carry it forth as I go about my day.

My older son, Ben, painted a beautiful picture of the shimmer for me as a gift to use in meditation. He calls it *God in the Sea* and says it symbolizes that any seeker "can experience the beauty and majesty of God that is present here on Earth and encircles us every day." That is the beauty and the holiness of the shimmer, Nature's gift to help us remember who we truly are. Shimmer on, sweet soul.

ॐ

Hymn to Beauty

By Nancy Stetson

all praise to

babies' buddha bellies

soft kitten tummies

and dogs rolling on their backs

in ecstasy

because you're rubbing the right spot

just below their heart.

i sing of

manhole covers

and neon at night

lone saxophone players on subway platforms

the sound of car tires

on city streets

when it rains.

all night diners

putting the kettle on

cupping a cup of coffee

while watching the rain

through the window.

it is beautiful

it is all beautiful

the sound of stilettos walking across a room

the curve of breast and hip

the smile

the throaty laugh

the aqua blue of the gulf

touching the baby blue of sky

the pillow under my head

at night

the enveloping comfort of

midnight darkness

pulled around me like a quilt

the book in my hand

the book in my heart

the words i am birthing

still giving shape to

the light in the window

the handwritten letter

read again and again.

i sing of my own unexpected beauty

and of yours

it is beautiful

it is all beautiful

☙

Beauty

By Deborah Svec-Carstens

"You can fall in love at first sight
with a place as with a person."
—Alec Waugh

God is everywhere. I learned this phrase as a child during summer vacation Bible school. But it took years before I really knew what it meant to experience God's presence all around. And, of course, I often forget this simple truth I have carried in my bones since childhood. I forget to pay attention and look around me, to find God in the every day. Sometimes it takes time away from daily routines to remember.

Having traveled to many places in my life, I never had the experience of love at first sight with a place until I set eyes on Glacier National Park in Montana. A circle of women spent a week experiencing God at Glacier—

hiking, laughing, resting, reflecting. The story of Scenic Point—our first hike of the week, and by far the most challenging—illustrates what I carry with me from Glacier.

***

The rocks crack under my feet like broken glass. Forced to pay attention to each step, everything else falls away. I see only the path immediately before me and the beauty that surrounds—mountains, trees, snow, flowers, rocks, amazingly clear blue sky. We began not knowing precisely the challenge before us. If we had known, none of us may have even started the journey. At each turn, we approach the top—and yet still so far to go. The last stretch as we head to the point, a quilt of purple and yellow flowers line our path. Finally at the top where amazing vistas await our arrival, I look out over the landscape, able to see at least 100 miles—the sky does not end, the day clear, cool and breezy—I am standing at the top of the mountain with the wind blowing, feeling God's presence.

My physical body speaks to me up and down the mountain. The pain in my knees is nearly unbearable on the way down. And just when I think I can't make it another step, one of my companions stops with me to rest. Grace. I want to break down and cry as we arrive at our last resting spot, where several from the group had been waiting for the slow ones before our final descent. Cussing, crying, focusing on the path before me. And, remembering to take a moment from time to time to look up, look around and breathe it all in.

I made it to the top of a mountain, carried by my own two feet. My shoulders and back held my backpack, filled with water, nourishment, layers of clothing. My hands carried my hiking poles, helping me to balance and work my way to the top. My knees guided me down the mountain, in spite of the pain. The physical body endured, carrying me to vistas I could not imagine, I cannot begin to describe. Trust.

***

I experienced God in many ways at Glacier, in the wind and the water, in the rainbows, in the vastness of the sky, in the flowers, the trees, in the beauty of the landscape; in the women accompanying me on the journey and in others that we interacted with during the week. The photos and my memories remind me of God's presence, here and now, all around. They remind me to pay attention, to open my eyes, to see again. Beauty.

꙳

Contributor Biographies

KATHLEEN ADAMS is a psychiatric nurse practitioner specializing in the care of children and adolescents. She lives in Des Moines, Iowa, with her best friend Randy. Her adult son Chris is an accomplished cellist. In her play time Kathy creates with fabric, dabbles with words and pedals the bike trails of central Iowa.

RONDA ARMSTRONG'S stories have appeared at http://womensmemoirs.com and in *Chicken Soup for the Soul* books. She rotates with other writers at http://thebridgemeditations.wordpress.com. When not writing, she dances with her husband or connects with family and friends.

VALERIE D. BENKO is a communications specialist from Western Pennsylvania who spends her free time writing about life. She has had more than a dozen stories published in the U.S. and Canada and is a frequent contributor to *Chicken Soup for the Soul*. Visit her online at http://valeriebenko.weebly.com.

BECCA BRISCOE (aka Peanut Beranksi) leads a blissful life in total subservience to her 4-year-old Maltese, Zoey. She is a retired local government bureaucrat in Northern

Indiana and considers herself richly blessed to be able to laugh at herself and the quirkiness of our human condition.

MARY CARTLEDGEHAYES is the author of three books, including *Semisweetness and Light* published by GoldenTree Communications. A well-known humorist, she offers mentoring services for writers in transition and workshops on writing authentically.

CAROLINE A. CATALDO is a 2012 graduate of the College of the Holy Cross, where she studied English, Creative Writing and anthropology. After graduation, she served for a year on the Crow Native American Reservation with the Jesuit Corps Northwest. Caroline will be attending Medill Northwestern University in the fall of 2013 as she pursues an M.S. in journalism.

ANGELA RAE CLARK describes herself as a "Tending Your Inner Garden Seedling still finding her way in the Inner Garden world." Her writing shares part of her 2011 experience of healing from repressed memories of rape, torture and trauma involving her grandfather. She offers others support and healing through her healing arts practice, The Ki Inside. www.TheKiInside.com

SUZANNE C. COLE is a retired college instructor with an M.A. from Stanford University. Her essays have been published in *Newsweek, Houston Chronicle, San Antonio Express-News, Baltimore Sun* and many anthologies, including two previous Inner Gardener books. She also writes poetry and short fiction and plays in a studio in the Texas Hill Country.

TASNEEM DAMJI is a mother to a beautiful boy who is inspiring her to get out of her comfort zone, take risks and above all, be true to herself. She moved with her family across the world to live a life of authenticity, simplicity and gratitude. She blogs at http://tasneem-damji.blog spot.com.

STACIA DUVALL is a writer, photographer and blogger who lives in Colorado. Her work explores the beauty of place and the lessons of time and appears in two blogs (Winsomebella and Through the Lens of We) and in various publications as well.

TERRI ELDERS, L.C.S.W., lives near Colville, Washington. Her stories have appeared in dozens of periodicals and anthologies. She is the in-house copy editor for Publishing Syndicate and co-creator of its anthology, *Not Your Mother's Book: On Travel.* Contact her at telders@hotmail.com and read her blog at http://atouchoftarragon.blogspot.com/.

MADDY STELLA FLETCHER was born in Ottawa, Canada. She currently divides her time between taming the wilds of the west and finding excuses to sleep in. She has never been successful but knows she would be great at it. She writes because she must.

MICHELLE J. FOSTER is an artist, writer and consultant in Paeonian Springs, Virginia. Her passions include art, gardening, literature, family and her animals. A former Knight International Journalism Fellow and corporate executive, she travels frequently and has lived in Cambodia, China, and Taiwan and Southeast Asia.

PATRICIA AMBROSE GRIFFIN of Lexington, Kentucky, is mother to three adult children and lovingly called Grandma by Sophia, Joshua and Jacob. Pat's passions include spiritual growth, discerning life choices and envisioning new beginnings. She began writing as a teenager who kept her diary under lock and key. Her current gypsy journey can be followed at http://pag213.wordpress.com.

CATHY AJ HARDY is an award-winning singer-songwriter/poet living in Mission, B.C., Canada. Deeply connected to the land where she lives and rooted in a deep spirituality, Cathy expresses her soul journey through song and spoken word. www.cathyajhardy.com

MIYOKO HIKIJI believes that words build worlds. As a student of life, she seeks to uncover the treasures of everyday life in places near and far, especially within. Miyoko is author of *All I Could Be: My Story as a Woman Warrior in Iraq.* Her blog is at www.allicouldbe.com.

DEBORAH JANSEN lives in small-town Iowa and loves the varied people and places in her state. As a contributing writer to *The Iowan*, she's eager to find fresh ways to tell old stories or uncover new ones that haven't been told. She also enjoys her work as a life skills coach for adults with intellectual disabilities. jansen.deb@gmail.com.

PHYLLIS JARDINE is a retired nurse living in the Annapolis Valley of Nova Scotia with her husband Bud and black lab Morgan. Her stories have been aired on national radio and have been published in *A Cup of Comfort* and *Chicken Soup for the Soul* books, as well as in numerous magazines and anthologies. phyl.jardine@gmail.com

BARBARA KNIGHT KATZ, PH.D., has taught Constitutional Law and Political Philosophy for most of her career. With an M.S. in Pastoral Counseling, she works with her church's pastoral care team. Family, a Shenandoah River cabin, Ireland and writing are among her delights. Her poems have appeared in *Sacred Journey* and *Piedmont Virginian.*

KIRSTEN LABLANC is a transplanted Iowan originally from Denver, Colorado. This writer, mother and spouse recently contributed to an eBook, *Love Poems Deconstructed: A Poetry Collection* and is currently working on a book documenting her grandparents' oral history. Kirsten blogs at eatingneonyogurt.com, exploring motherhood and faith.

SHARON MEIXSELL resides in Kenmore, Washington. She finds happiness in writing poetry. Her poem "In the Fog" was published in *Di-verse-city: 2013 Austin International Poetry Festival Anthology.* Sharon's poetry is also found in a book she co-authored, titled *Spirit Rocks* (Poetica Publishing, August 2012).

GERI MORAN is a technical writer and craft artist who lives in New York. She loves to make people smile with her handcrafted products and monthly blog. Her deepest happiness comes from being with her wonderful friends and family, and from visiting Mystic, Connecticut.

JEAN NAVIAUX is retired from teaching English in Miami and currently is teaching herself how to write. Along with "thinking" about writing a memoir, she enjoys reading, drinking wine, learning Spanish and traveling to exotic places with her boyfriend of 35 years.

ANN QUID has been writing in a variety of fields for 45 years. Her poems have been published in several countries in anthologies and periodicals, including *Scintilla, California Quarterly, Tamba, Carillon* and *Tree Magic/ Nature's Antennas.* A chatbook was author-published in 2001. A volume of poetry and photography is in the mill.

RACHEL C. REGENOLD is a seeker, writer and yoga practitioner in Des Moines, Iowa, where she lives with her four-legged children.

ANGELA RENKOSKI is set to graduate in August 2013 from the master's program in spiritual psychology at the University of Santa Monica. She cherishes her sons, Ben and Nick, and daughters-in-law Julie and Liz. Her most recent project is developing a writing workshop around three of her favorite things: myth, music and metaphor.

CELESTE SNOWBER, PH.D., is a dancer, poet and educator who is an Associate Professor in the Faculty of Education in the area of Arts Education at Simon Fraser

University outside Vancouver, B.C., Canada. She is author of *Embodied Prayer* and coauthor of *Landscapes of Aesthetic Education*. Her website is www.celestesnowber.com and her blog is www.bodypsalms.com.

NANCY STETSON, a native New Yorker, now is an arts and entertainment writer/critic for the Florida Weekly (www.floridaweekly.com). In 2008 the Alliance for the Arts awarded her an Angel of the Arts Award, naming her Arts Journalist of the Year. She currently is writing a memoir about the year she used music and books to get her through a time of great loss.

DEBORAH SVEC-CARSTENS lives in Iowa with her husband Mike. She enjoys spending time with her nieces and nephews, reading, writing, swimming, practicing yoga and hiking. Deborah shares her love of music singing with the Des Moines Choral Society.

LORI ULRICH is a poet with heart. She writes about nature, relationships and family. She believes there is a poem lurking around every corner, just asking to be written. She is an observer, a listener and a recorder. Lori finds inspiration in everything!

MARI WETTER was born in Philadelphia and spent summers on the Jersey shore. Currently she is a nationally certified counselor using art and horticulture to bring hope to clients. She lives with her husband, writer Bruce Wetter, and retired rodeo dog Lady Ann in Wallowa County, Oregon. Email her at mwetter@netzero.net.

SUSAN WILSON is a GOMO (Get Over it; Move On) coach, working with client teams to discover fast, effective solutions for more influential leadership, lasting team strength and goal achievement beyond expectation. GOMO is a powerful tool to Get Over obstacles that block success and Move On to remarkable achievements.

Discussion and Journaling Questions

When have you experienced pure joy? Faced a struggle and learned your strength? Celebrated your resilience? Sunk into the reality of the present moment? Savored beauty? At those times, you've witnessed the power of summer.

Use these essays and poems to jog your memories, uncover your insights, acknowledge your triumphs and recall your pleasures. Then pick up your pen and journal or go to your laptop and begin to free-write. Don't be concerned about what you say or how you say it. Give yourself the freedom to express whatever comes to mind.

Like our authors, you may be a beginner or a pro. Either way, you're invited to indulge yourself with a few minutes or hours of reflection and writing. If you're inclined to share, discover the power of telling someone else your story.

JOY
- When do you feel most alive?
- What totally absorbs your attention?
- What experiences as a child brought you total delight?
- How would an ideal day unfold and end?
- When is your body infused with energy?

STORMS
- What setbacks have you encountered in life?
- When did a much-anticipated event disappoint you?
- How did you feel during a particularly difficult time?
- Which life storms were out of your control?
- Which, in retrospect, might you have expected?

MINDFULNESS
- What activities or involvements require your total attention?
- When are you totally present to nature?
- How and when do you engage in childlike curiosity?
- What memories will stay etched in your mind?
- How does it feel to notice something in exquisite detail?

RESILIENCE

- What have you learned from a life challenge?
- How does resilience express itself in your life?
- What helps you to recover and move ahead?
- How and when have you been courageous?
- What wisdom do you have to offer?

BEAUTY

- What attracts you and calls for your total attention?
- How do your senses allow you to experience beauty?
- How are you beautiful?
- In what way is beauty a spiritual experience?
- How does each season express its beauty to you?

❧

THE TENDING YOUR INNER GARDEN® program invites you to discover your deeper self and your relationship with all that is sacred. Using the seasons as a model for change, we help you develop a spiritual practice, tuning in to your own inner guidance so you can live in alignment with your true self. Tending Your Inner Garden® seeks to ...

- Bring women together in community.
- Celebrate each woman's unique expression of creativity.
- Support and nurture spiritual growth for each woman.
- Encourage women to discover, create and extend the fullest expression of who they are.
- Encourage entrepreneurial efforts by women to improve the health and well-being of the Earth.

www.tendingyourinnergarden.com